Contents

What is a magnet? 4

Magnetic or non-magnetic? 6

Magnetic metals 8

Shapes of magnets 10

Test of strength 12

Using magnets 14

Magnets at home 16

Compasses 18

Magnetic poles 20

Poles that attract 22

Poles that push each other away . . 24

Magnetized! 26

Making a magnet 28

Glossary 30

Answers 31

Index 32

Any words appearing in the text in bold, **like this**,
are explained in the Glossary.

What is a magnet?

A magnet is something that can pull some things towards it. The magnet has a **force** in it that you cannot see. You can only see what it does.

My World of Science

MAGNETS

Angela Royston

Heinemann
LIBRARY

www.heinemann.co.uk/library
Visit our website to find out more information about **Heinemann Library** books.

To order:
☎ Phone 44 (0) 1865 888066
▤ Send a fax to 44 (0) 1865 314091
▭ Visit the Heinemann Bookshop at www.heinemann.co.uk/library to browse our catalogue and order online.

First published in Great Britain by Heinemann Library, Halley Court, Jordan Hill, Oxford, OX2 8EJ, a division of Reed Educational & Professional Publishing Ltd. Heinemann is a registered trademark of Reed Educational & Professional Publishing Ltd.

OXFORD   MELBOURNE   AUCKLAND   JOHANNESBURG   BLANTYRE
GABORONE   IBADAN   PORTSMOUTH NH (USA)   CHICAGO

Designed by bigtop, Bicester, UK
Originated by Ambassador Litho Ltd.
Printed and bound in Hong Kong/China

06 05 04 03 02   06 05 04 03 02
10 9 8 7 6 5 4 3 2   10 9 8 7 6 5 4 3 2 1

ISBN 0 431 13704 8 (hardback)   ISBN 0 431 13710 2 (paperback)

British Library Cataloguing in Publication Data
Royston, Angela
Magnets. – (My world of science)
1. Magnets – Juvenile literature
I. Title
538.4

Acknowledgements
The Publishers would like to thank the following for permission to reproduce photographs:
Photodisc: p14; Powerstock Photo Library: p15; Stockshot: p18; Trevor Clifford: pp4, 5, 6, 7, 8, 10, 11, 12, 13, 16, 17, 19, 20, 21, 22, 23, 24, 25, 26, 27, 28, 29; Trip: M Barlow p9.

Cover photograph reproduced with permission of Robert Harding.

Every effort has been made to contact copyright holders of any material reproduced in this book. Any omissions will be rectified in subsequent printings if notice is given to the Publisher.

This fishing rod has a magnet tied to the end of the line. The magnet pulls the fish towards it. How many fish has the magnet picked up?

Magnetic or non-magnetic?

Magnets only work on some kinds of **materials**. If something is pulled towards a magnet, it is said to be **magnetic**. A paper clip is magnetic.

The leaf is non-magnetic because the magnet cannot lift it. You can use a magnet to test whether something is magnetic or non-magnetic.

Magnetic metals

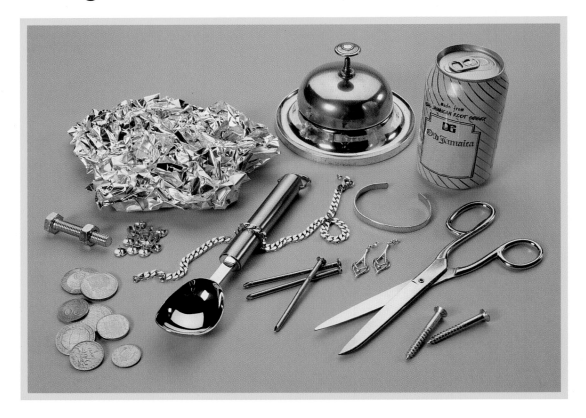

Metals are hard, strong and shiny.
There are many different metals. All the
things in the picture are made of metal.
Only some metals are **magnetic**.

Iron and steel are metals that are magnetic. Iron and steel are used to make many things, including trains, bridges and paper clips.

Shapes of magnets

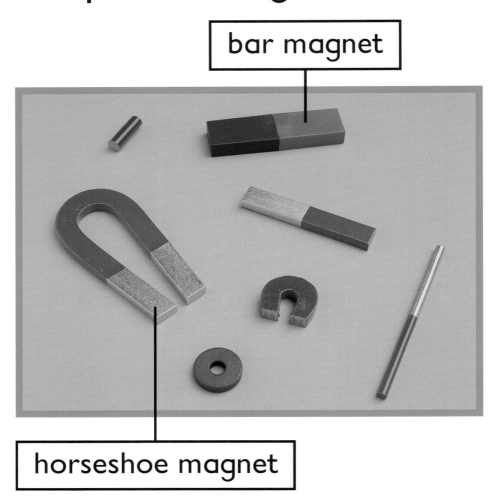

bar magnet

horseshoe magnet

Magnets can be any **shape**. The two most common shapes for magnets are a horseshoe and a bar.

The shapes that stick to your fridge have a small magnet on the back. The magnets stick to the door of the fridge because it is made of steel.

Test of strength

This girl is testing which magnet is stronger. She puts a nail on a line on a piece of paper. Then she moves the first magnet slowly towards the nail.

When the nail moves to the magnet, she marks where the magnet is. She does the same for the next magnet. The strongest magnet pulls the nail furthest.

Using magnets

A **recycling centre** uses magnets to separate aluminium cans from steel cans. Only the steel cans are **attracted** to the magnets.

Magnets are used to move heavy lumps of metal. This crane has a huge magnet on the end. It lifts the scrap metal.

Magnets at home

The knives in the picture are sticking to a **magnetic** knife-holder. What metal do you think the knives are made of?

The door of a fridge has a rubber strip covering a magnet. The magnet under the rubber sticks to the steel fridge. It keeps the door tightly closed.

rubber strip

Compasses

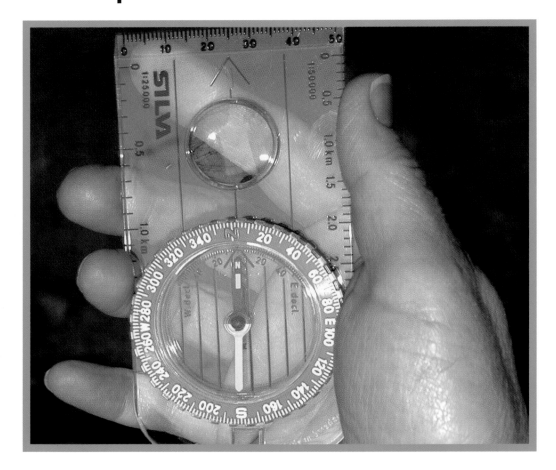

A compass uses a magnet to tell you what direction you are going in. The compass needle always points north. Hikers and sailors use compasses.

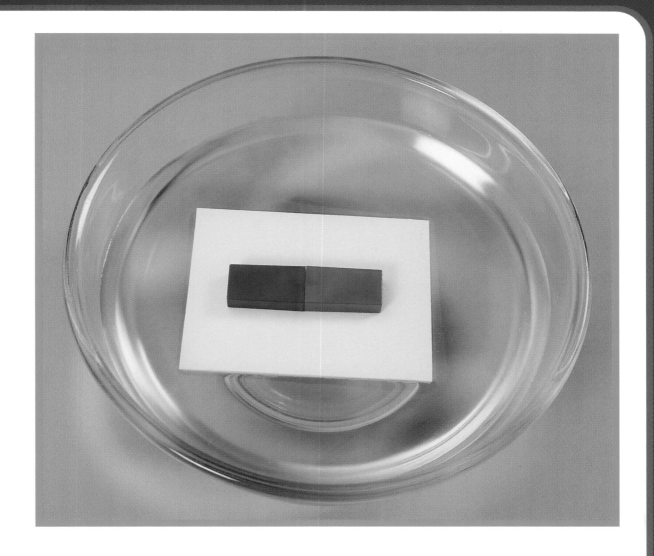

This is a home-made compass. It floats and can turn on the water. One end of the magnet points north and the other end points south.

Magnetic poles

This magnet was placed on top of a pile of pins. The strongest parts of the magnet pick up the most pins. Which is stronger – the ends or the middle?

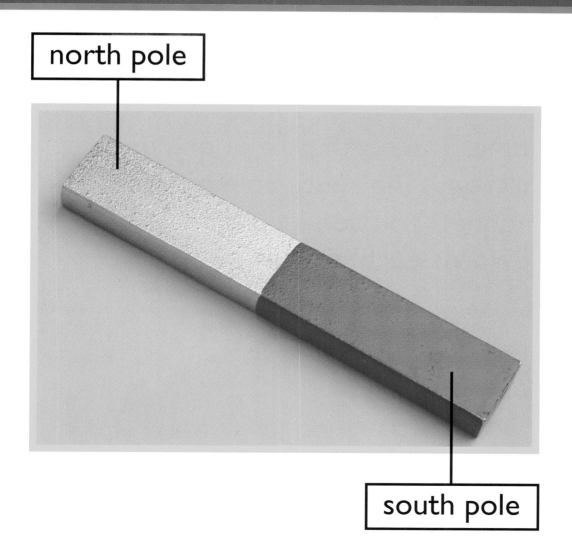

north pole

south pole

The ends of a magnet are called the poles. One end is called the north pole and the other end the south pole.

Poles that attract

The two poles of a magnet are not the same. The north pole of one magnet **attracts** the south pole of another magnet. You can feel them pulling towards each other.

| north pole | south pole |

The attraction is very strong.
Sometimes it can be hard to pull the
magnets apart!

Poles that push each other away

Sometimes magnets **repel** each other. However hard you try, you cannot make a north pole stick to another north pole. Two south poles also repel each other.

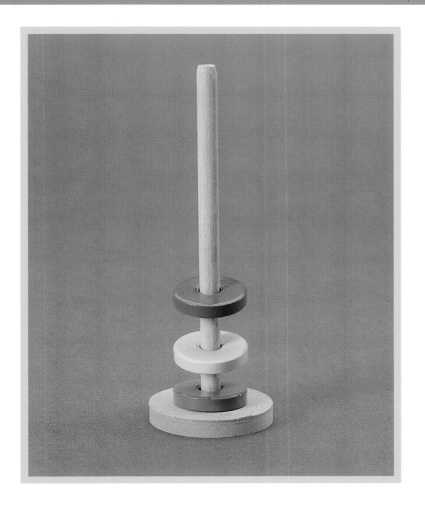

These magnets are floating above
each other! The poles are at the top
and bottom of the ring magnets.
They are pushing each other away.

Magnetized!

When iron or steel sticks to a magnet, it becomes magnetized. This means it becomes a magnet too. The first paper clip magnetizes the second paper clip.

The stronger the magnet, the longer the chain of paper clips. But if you remove the magnet, the chain falls apart. The paper clips are no longer magnetized.

Making a magnet

You can make a magnet that lasts. This boy is stroking a nail with a magnet. He strokes it about 50 times, in the same direction.

The nail becomes a magnet too. It is strong enough to pick up this paper clip. Now you can make lots of magnets!

Glossary

attract pull towards something

force power that makes things move

magnetic something that can be pulled towards a magnet

material what something is made of

recycling centre place where used glass and metal and other things are made into new things

repel push away from something

shape the form that things take – for example, a square or a circle

Answers

Page 5 – What is a magnet?
The magnet has picked up two fish.

Page 16 – Magnets at home
The knives are made of steel.

Page 20 – Magnetic poles
The ends of the magnet are stronger.

Index

bar magnets 10

crane 15

fridge magnets 11

fridges 11, 17

home-made compass 19

horseshoe magnets 10

iron 9, 26

knife-holders 16

magnetic materials 6, 8–9, 16, 17

magnetizing 26–29

non-magnetic materials 7

paper clips 6, 9, 26–27, 29

poles of a magnet 20–25

recyling centre 14

steel 9, 11, 14, 26

testing magnets 12–13